My First
UKRAINIAN
DICTIONARY

ENGLISH-UKRAINIAN

Designed and edited by Maria Watson
Translated by Katerina Volobuyeva

Hippocrene Books, Inc.
New York

My First Ukrainian Dictionary

English-Ukrainian

Hippocrene Books, Inc. edition, 2023

For information, address:
HIPPOCRENE BOOKS, INC.
171 Madison Avenue
New York, NY 10016
www.hippocrenebooks.com

ISBN: 978-0-7818-1442-3

First edition, 2023

Published by arrangement with Biblio Bee Publications, an imprint of ibs Books (UK)
56, Langland Crescent, Stanmore HA7 1NG, U.K.

Printed at Everest Press, New Delhi-110 020 (India)

Aa

actor

актор

aktor

actress

акторка

aktorka

adult

дорослий

doroslyi

aeroplane

US English **airplane**

аероплан

aeroplan

air conditioner

кондиціонер

kondytsioner

air hostess

US English **flight attendant**

стюардеса

stiuardesa

airport

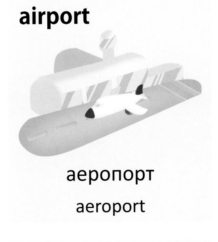

аеропорт

aeroport

album

альбом

albom

almond

мигдаль

myhdal

alphabet

абетка

abetka

ambulance

швидка допомога

shvydka dopomoha

angel

янгол

yanhol

animal

тварина

tvaryna

ankle

щиколотка

shchykolotka

ant

мураха

murakha

antelope

антилопа

antylopa

antenna

антена

antena

apartment

квартира

kvartyra

ape

мавпа

mavpa

apple

яблуко

yabluko

apricot

абрикос

abrykos

apron

фартух

fartukh

aquarium

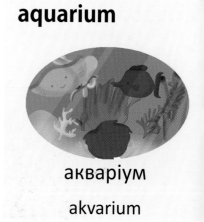

акваріум

akvarium

archery

стрільба з лука

strilba z luka

architect

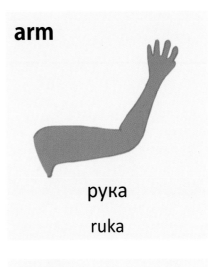

архітектор

arkhitektor

arm

рука

ruka

armour
US English **armor**

обладунки

obladunky

arrow

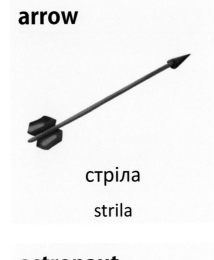

стріла

strila

artist

художник

khudozhnyk

asparagus

спаржа

sparzha

astronaut

астронавт

astronavt

astronomer

астроном

astronom

athlete

спортсмен

sportsmen

atlas

атлас

atlas

aunt

тітка

titka

a
b
c
d
e
f
g
h
i
J
k
l
m
n
o
p
q
r
s
t
u
v
w
x
y
z

author

автор

avtor

automobile

автомобіль

avtomobil

autumn
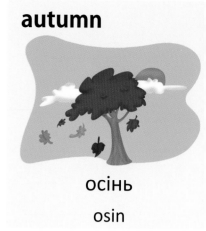
осінь

osin

avalanche

лавина

lavyna

award

нагорода

nahoroda

axe

сокира

sokyra

Bb

baby

немовля

nemovlia

back

спина

spyna

bacon

бекон

bekon

badge

значок

znachok

badminton

бадмінтон

badminton

bag

торба

torba

baker

пекар

pekar

balcony

балкон

balkon

bald

лисина

lysyna

ball

м'яч

m'iach

ballerina

балерина

baleryna

balloon

повітряна кулька

povitriana kulka

bamboo

бамбук

bambuk

banana

банан

banan

band

оркестр

orkestr

bandage

пов'язка

pov'iazka

barbeque

барбекю

barbekiu

barn

амбар

ambar

barrel

діжка

dizhka

baseball

бейсбол

beisbol

basket

кошик

koshyk

basketball

баскетбол

basketbol

bat

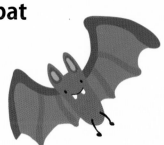

кажан

kazhan

bath

ванна

vanna

battery

BATTERY

батарейка

batareika

bay

бухта

bukhta

beach

пляж

pliazh

beak

дзьоб

dzob

bean

біб

bib

bear

ведмідь

vedmid

beard

борода

boroda

bed

ліжко

lizhko

bee

бджола

bdzhola

beetle

жук

zhuk

beetroot

буряк

buriak

bell

дзвінок

dzvinok

belt

пас

pas

berry

ягода

yahoda

bicycle

велосипед

velosyped

billiards
US English **pool**

більярд

biliard

bin

кошик для сміття

koshyk dlia smittia

a
b
c
d
e
f
g
h
i
J
K
l
m
n
o
p
q
r
s
t
u
v
w
x
y
z

bird

птах

ptakh

biscuit

печиво

pechyvo

black

чорний колір

chornyi kolir

blackboard

шкільна дошка

shkilna doshka

blanket

ковдра

kovdra

blizzard

заметіль

zametil

blood

кров

krov

blue

синій колір

synii kolir

boat

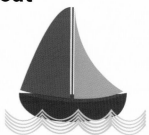

човен

choven

body

тіло

tilo

bone

кістка

kistka

book

книга

knyha

boot

чоботи

choboty

bottle

пляшка

pliashka

bow

бант

bant

bowl

миска

myska

box

коробка

korobka

boy

хлопчик

khlopchyk

bracelet

браслет

braslet

brain
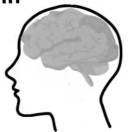

мозок

mozok

branch

гілка

hilka

bread

хліб

khlib

breakfast

сніданок

snidanok

brick

цеглина

tsehlyna

a
b
c
d
e
f
g
h
i
J
K
l
m
n
o
p
q
r
s
t
u
v
w
x
y
z

bride

наречена
narechena

bridegroom

наречений
narechenyi

bridge

міст
mist

broom

помело
pomelo

brother

брат
brat

brown

коричневий колір
korychnevyi kolir

brush

пензель
penzel

bubble

бульбашка
bulbashka

bucket

відро
vidro

buffalo

буйвол
buivol

building

будівля
budivlia

bulb

лампочка
lampochka

bull

бик

byk

bun

булка

bulka

bunch

букет

buket

bundle

купа

kupa

bungalow

бунгало

bunhalo

burger

бургер

burher

bus

автобус

avtobus

bush

кущ

kushch

butcher

м'ясник

m'iasnyk

butter

масло

maslo

butterfly

метелик

metelyk

button

ґудзик

gudzyk

a
b
c
d
e
f
g
h
i
j
J
k
l
m
n
o
p
q
r
s
t
u
v
w
x
y
z

Cc

cabbage

капуста

kapusta

cabinet

шафа

shafa

cable

кабель

kabel

cable car

канатна дорога

kanatna doroha

cactus

кактус

kaktus

cafe

кав'ярня

kav'iarnia

cage

клітка

klitka

cake

пиріг

pyrih

calculator

калькулятор

kalkuliator

calendar

календар

kalendar

calf

теля

telia

camel

верблюд

verbliud

camera

фотоаппарат

fotoaparat

camp

табір

tabir

can

банка

banka

canal

канал

kanal

candle

свічка

svichka

canoe

каное

kanoe

canteen

їдальня

yidalnia

cap

кашкет

kashket

captain

капітан

kapitan

car

автомобіль

avtomobil

caravan

фургон

furhon

a b c d e f g h i J k l m n o p q r s t u v w x y z

a b c d e f g h i j k l m n o p q r s t u v w x y z

card

листівка

lystivka

carnival

карнавал

karnaval

carpenter

тесля

teslia

carpet

килим

kylym

carrot

морква

morkva

cart

тачка

tachka

cartoon

мультфільм

multfilm

cascade

водоспад

vodospad

castle
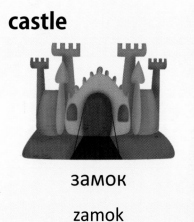
замок

zamok

cat
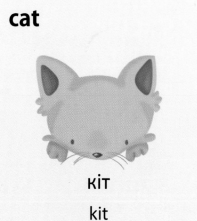
кіт

kit

caterpillar
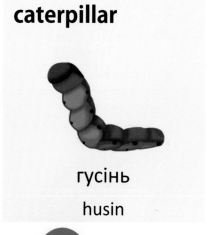
гусінь

husin

cauliflower

цвітна капуста

tsvitna kapusta

cave

печера

pechera

ceiling

стеля

stelia

centipede

сороконіжка

sorokonizhka

centre
US English **center**

центр

tsentr

cereal

крупа

krupa

chain

ланцюг

lantsiuh

chair

стілець

stilets

chalk

крейда

kreida

cheek

щока

shchoka

cheese

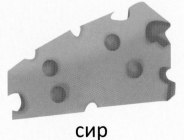

сир

syr

chef

шеф-кухар

shef-kukhar

cherry

вишня

vyshnia

a b **c** d e f g h i j J k l m n o p q r s t u v w x y z

chess

шахи
shakhy

chest

грудна клітина
hrudna klityna

chick

курча
kurcha

chilli
US English **chili**

чілі
chili

chimney

димохід
dymokhid

chin

підборіддя
pidboriddia

chocolate
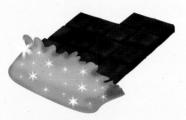
шоколад
shokolad

Christmas

Різдво
Rizdvo

church

церква
tserkva

cinema
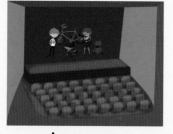
кінотеатр
kinoteatr

circle

коло
kolo

circus

цирк
tsyrk

city

місто

misto

classroom

класна кімната

klasna kimnata

clinic

клініка

klinika

clock

годинник

hodynnyk

cloth

серветка

servetka

cloud

хмара

khmara

clown

клоун

kloun

coal

вугілля

vuhillia

coast

узбережжя

uzberezhzhia

coat

пальто
palto

cobra

кобра
kobra

cockerel
US English **rooster**

півень
piven

a b **c** d e f g h i J k l m n o p q r s t u v w x y z

a b **c** d e f g h i j J k l m n o p q r s t u v w x y z

cockroach

тарган

tarhan

coconut

кокос

kokos

coffee

кава

kava

coin

монета

moneta

colour
US English **color**

колір

kolir

comb

гребінь

hrebin

comet

комета

kometa

compass

компас

kompas

computer

комп'ютер

komp'iuter

cone

конус

konus

container

контейнер

konteiner

cook

кухар

kukhar

cookie

печиво

pechyvo

cord

шнур

shnur

corn

кукурудза

kukurudza

cot

люлька

liulka

cottage

котедж

kotedzh

cotton

бавовна

bavovna

country

країна

kraina

couple

пара

para

court

суд

sud

cow
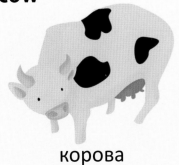
корова

korova

crab

краб

krab

crane

кран

kran

crayon

олівець

olivets

crocodile

крокодил

krokodyl

cross

хрест

khrest

crow

гава

hava

crowd

натовп

natovp

crown
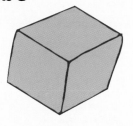
корона

korona

cube

куб

kub

cucumber

огірок

ohirok

cup

чашка

chashka

cupboard

кухонна шафа

kukhonna shafa

curtain

штора

shtora

cushion
подушка

podushka

Dd

dam

дамба

damba

dancer

танцюрист

tantsiuryst

dart

дротик

drotyk

data

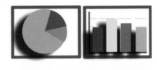

дані

dani

dates

фінік

finik

daughter

донька

donka

day

день

den

deck

колода

koloda

deer

олень

olen

den

лігво

lihvo

dentist

стоматолог

stomatoloh

desert

пустеля

pustelia

design

дизайн

dyzain

desk

письмовий стіл

pysmovyi stil

dessert

десерт

desert

detective

детектив

detektyv

diamond

діамант

diamant

diary

щоденник

shchodennyk

dice

гральний кубик

hralnyi kubyk

dictionary

словник

slovnyk

dinosaur

динозавр

dynozavr

disc

диск

dysk

dish

блюдо

bliudo

diver

дайвер

daiver

dock

пристань

prystan

doctor

лікар

likar

dog

пес

pes

doll

лялька

lialka

dolphin

дельфін

delfin

dome

купол

kupol

domino

доміно

domino

donkey

віслюк

visliuk

donut

пончик

ponchyk

door

двері

dveri

dough

тісто

tisto

dragon

дракон

drakon

drain

злив

zlyv

drawer

шухляда

shukhliada

drawing

малювання

maliuvannia

dream

сон

son

dress

сукня

suknia

drink

напій

napii

driver

водій

vodii

drop

крапля

kraplia

drought

засуха

zasukha

drum

барабан

baraban

duck

качка

kachka

dustbin
US English **trash can**

відро для сміття

vidro dlia smittia

duvet

простирадло

prostyradlo

dwarf

гном

gnom

Ee

eagle

орел

orel

ear

вухо

vukho

earring

сережка

serezhka

earth

Земля

Zemlia

earthquake

землетрус

zemletrus

earthworm

дощовий черв'як

doshchovyi cherv'iak

eclipse

затьмарення

zatmarennia

edge

край

krai

eel
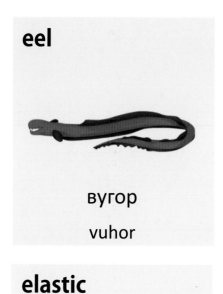
вугор

vuhor

egg
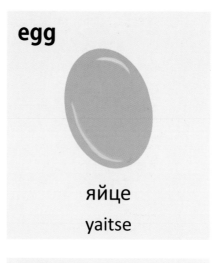
яйце

yaitse

eight

вісім

visim

elastic
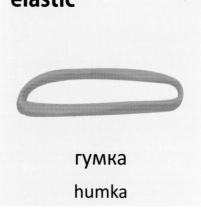
гумка

humka

elbow

лікоть

likot

electrician

електрик

elektryk

electricity

електрика

elektryka

elephant
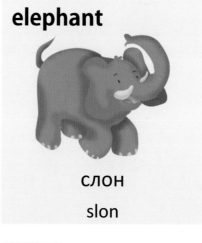
слон

slon

elevator

ліфт

lift

elf

ельф

elf

email

електронна пошта

elektronna poshta

embroidery

вишивання

vyshyvannia

engine

двигун

dvyhun

entrance
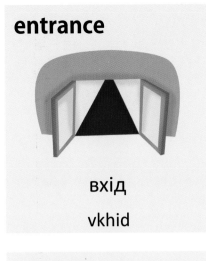
вхід

vkhid

envelope

конверт

konvert

equator

екватор

ekvator

equipment

устаткування

ustatkuvannia

eraser
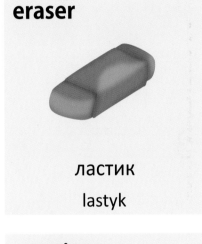
ластик

lastyk

escalator

ескалатор

eskalator

eskimo

ескімос

eskimos

evening

вечір

vechir

exhibition

виставка

vystavka

eye
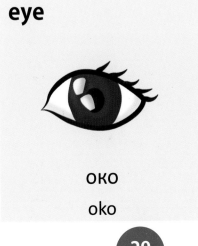
око

oko

eyebrow
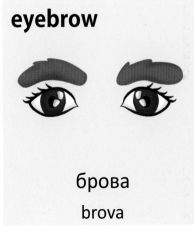
брова

brova

a b c d e f g h i j k l m n o p q r s t u v w x y z

Ff

fabric

тканина

tkanyna

face

лице

lytse

factory

фабрика

fabryka

fairy

фея

feia

family

родина

rodyna

fan

вентилятор

ventyliator

farm

ферма

ferma

farmer

фермер

fermer

fat

гладкий

hladkyi

father

батько

batko

feather

пір'я

pir'ia

female

жінка

zhinka

fence

паркан

parkan

ferry

паром

parom

field

поле

pole

fig

інжир

inzhyr

file

тека

teka

film

плівка

plivka

finger

палець

palets

fire

вогонь

vohon

fire engine

пожежна машина

pozhezhna mashyna

fire fighter

пожежник

pozhezhnyk

fireworks

феєрверки

feierverky

fish

риба

ryba

fist

кулак

kulak

five
5
п'ять

p'iat

flag

прапор

prapor

flame

полум'я

polum'ia

flamingo

фламінго

flaminho

flask

фляжка

fliazhka

flock

отара

otara

flood

повінь

povin

floor
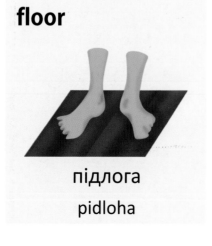
підлога

pidloha

florist

флорист

floryst

flour

борошно

boroshno

flower

квітка

kvitka

flute

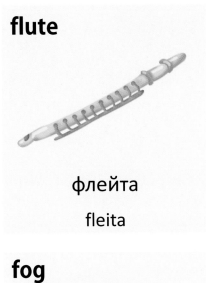

флейта

fleita

fly

муха

mukha

foam

піна

pina

fog

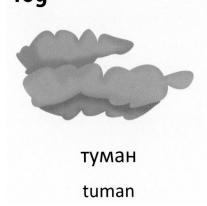

туман

tuman

foil

фольга

folha

food

їжа

yizha

foot

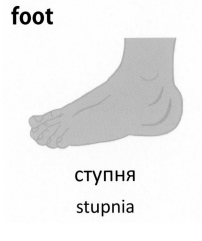

ступня

stupnia

football

US English **soccer**

футбол

futbol

forearm

передпліччя

peredplichchia

forehead

лоб

lob

forest

ліс

lis

fork

виделка

vydelka

fortress

фортеця

fortetsia

fountain

фонтан

fontan

four

чотири

chotyry

fox

лисиця

lysytsia

frame

рама

rama

freezer

морозильна камера

morozylna kamera

fridge
US English **refrigerator**

холодильник

kholodylnyk

friend

друг

druh

frog

жаба

zhaba

fruit

фрукт

frukt

fumes

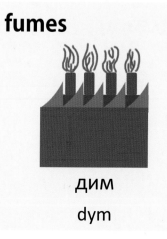

дим

dym

funnel

лійка

liika

furnace

піч

pich

furniture

меблі

mebli

Gg

gadget

пристрій

prystrii

gallery

галерея

halereia

game

гра

hra

gap

проміжок

promizhok

garage

гараж

harazh

garbage

сміття

smittia

garden

сад

sad

garland

гірлянда

hirlianda

garlic

часник

chasnyk

gas

газ

haz

gate

брама

brama

gem

дорогоцінне каміння

dorohotsinne kaminnia

generator

генератор

henerator

germ

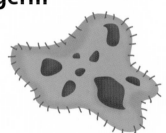

мікроб

mikrob

geyser

гейзер

heizer

ghost

привид

pryvyd

giant

велетень

veleten

gift

подарунок

podarunok

ginger

імбир

imbyr

giraffe

жирафа

zhyrafa

girl

дівчинка

divchynka

glacier

льодовик

lodovyk

glass

скло

sklo

glider

планер

planer

globe

глобус

hlobus

glove

рукавичка

rukavychka

glue

клей

klei

goal

ворота

vorota

goat

коза

koza

gold

золото

zoloto

golf

гольф

holf

goose

гусак

husak

a
b
c
d
e
f
g
h
i
J
k
l
m
n
o
p
q
r
s
t
u
v
w
x
y
z

gorilla

горила

horyla

grain

зерно

zerno

grandfather

дідусь

didus

grandmother

бабуся

babusia

grape

виноград

vynohrad

grapefruit

грейпфрут

hreipfrut

grass

трава

trava

grasshopper

коник

konyk

gravel

гравій

hravii

green

зелений колір

zelenyi kolir

grey

сірий колір

siryi kolir

grill

гриль

hryl

grocery

овочі

ovochi

ground

ґрунт

grunt

guard

охоронець

okhoronets

guava

ґуава

guava

guide

гід

hid

guitar

гітара

hitara

gulf

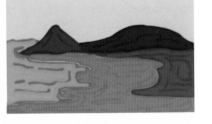

затока

zatoka

gun

зброя

zbroia

gypsy

циган

tsyhan

Hh

hair

волосся

volossia

hairbrush

щітка для волосся

shchitka dlia volossia

a b c d e f g h i j k l m n o p q r s t u v w x y z

hairdresser

перукар

perukar

half

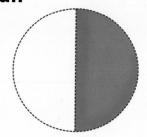

половина

polovyna

hall

зала

zala

ham

шинка

shynka

hammer

молоток

molotok

hammock

гамак

hamak

hand

рука

ruka

handbag

сумочка

sumochka

handicraft

ремесло

remeslo

handkerchief

хусточка

khustochka

handle

ручка

ruchka

hanger

вішак

vishak

harbour
US English **harbor**

гавань

havan

hare

заєць

zaiets

harvest

урожай

urozhai

hat

капелюх

kapeliukh

hawk

яструб

yastrub

hay

сіно

sino

head

голова

holova

headphone

навушники

navushnyky

heap

купа

kupa

heart

серце

sertse

heater

обігрівач

obihrivach

hedge

живопліт

zhyvoplit

a b c d e f g h i J K l m n o p q r s t u v w x y z

heel

підбор

pidbor

helicopter

гелікоптер

helikopter

helmet

шолом

sholom

hen

курка

kurka

herb

трави

travy

herd

стадо

stado

hermit

відлюдник

vidliudnyk

hill

пагорб

pahorb

hippopotamus
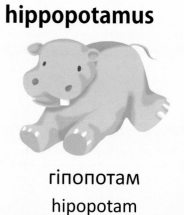
гіпопотам

hipopotam

hive
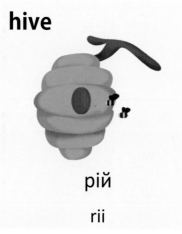
рій

rii

hole

дірка

dirka

honey

мед

med

hood

капюшон
kapiushon

hook

гак
hak

horn

ріг
rih

horse

кінь
kin

hose

шланг
shlanh

hospital

лікарня
likarnia

hotdog

хот-дог
khot-doh

hotel

готель
hotel

hour

година
hodyna

house

будинок
budynok

human

людина
liudyna

hunter

мисливець
myslyvets

hurricane

ураган

urahan

husband

чоловік

cholovik

hut

хатинка

khatynka

Ii

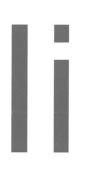

ice

лід

lid

iceberg

айсберг

aisberh

ice cream

морозиво

morozyvo

idol
ідол

idol

igloo
іглу

ihlu

inch

дюйм

diuim

injection

ін'єкція

in'iektsiia

injury

травма

travma

ink

чорнило

chornylo

inn

таверна

taverna

insect

комаха

komakha

inspector

інспектор

inspektor

instrument

інструмент

instrument

internet

Інтернет

Internet

intestine

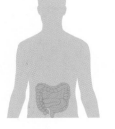

кишечник

kyshechnyk

inventor

винахідник

vynakhidnyk

invitation

запрошення

zaproshennia

iron

праска

praska

island

острів

ostriv

ivory

слонова кістка

slonova kistka

a b c d e f g h i **J** j k l m n o p q r s t u v w x y z

Jj

jackal

шакал

shakal

jacket

куртка

kurtka

jackfruit

джекфрут

dzhekfrut

jam

варення

varennia

jar

банка

banka

javelin

спис

spys

jaw

щелепа

shchelepa

jeans

джинси

dzhynsy

jelly

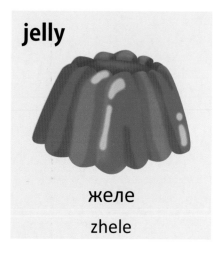

желе

zhele

jetty

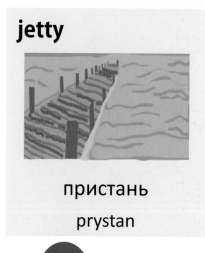

пристань

prystan

jewellery

US English **jewelry**

прикраси

prykrasy

jigsaw

головоломка

holovolomka

jockey

жокей

zhokei

joker

жартівник

zhartivnyk

journey

подорож

podorozh

jug

глек

hlek

juggler

жонглер

zhonhler

juice

сік

sik

jungle

джунглі

dzhunhli

jute

джут

dzhut

Kk

kangaroo

кенгуру

kenhuru

kennel

будка

budka

kerb
US English **curb**

узбіччя

uzbichchia

kerosene

гас

has

ketchup

кетчуп

ketchup

kettle

чайник

chainyk

key

ключ

kliuch

keyboard

клавіатура

klaviatura

key ring

кільце для ключів

kiltse dlia kliuchiv

kidney

нирка

nyrka

kilogram

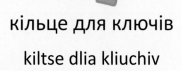

кілограм

kilohram

king

король

korol

kiosk

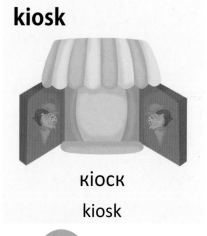

кіоск

kiosk

kiss

поцілунок

potsilunok

kitchen

кухня

kukhnia

kite

повітряний змій

povitrianyi zmii

kitten

кошеня

koshenia

kiwi

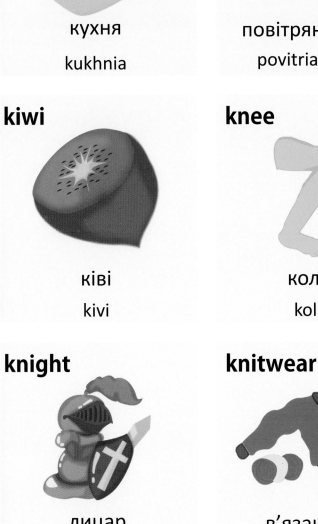

ківі

kivi

knee

коліно

kolino

knife

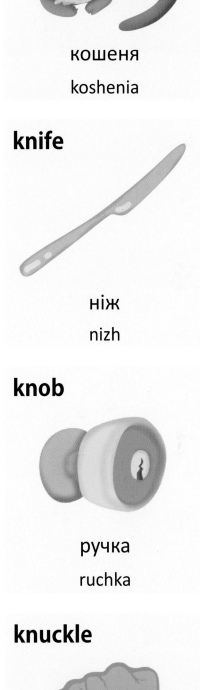

ніж

nizh

knight

лицар

lytsar

knitwear

в'язані речі

v'iazani rechi

knob

ручка

ruchka

knock

стук

stuk

knot

вузол

vuzol

knuckle

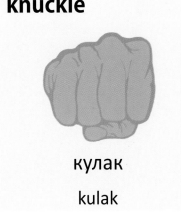

кулак

kulak

Ll

label

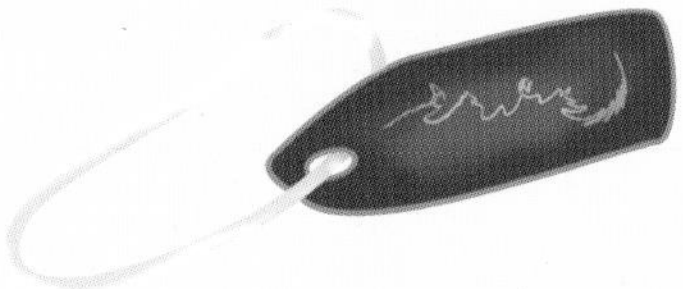

бирка

byrka

laboratory

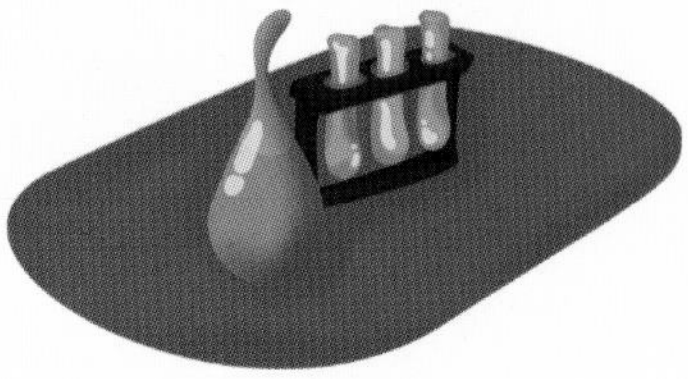

лабораторія

laboratoriia

lace

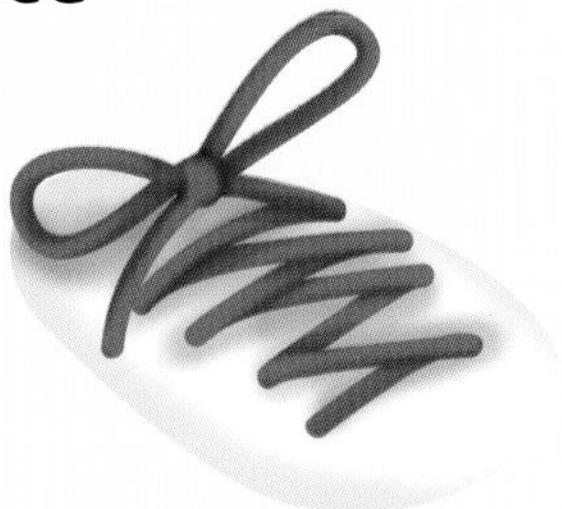

шнурки

shnurky

ladder

драбина

drabyna

lady

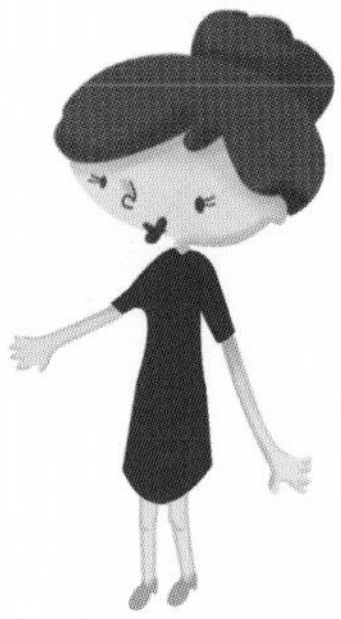

леді

ledi

ladybird
US English **ladybug**

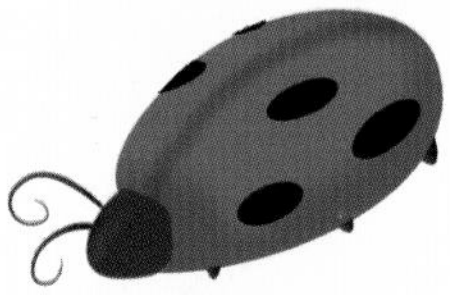

сонечко

sonechko

lagoon

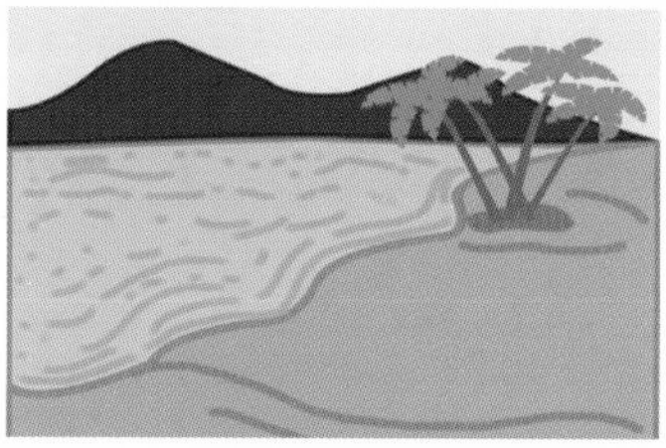

лагуна

lahuna

lake

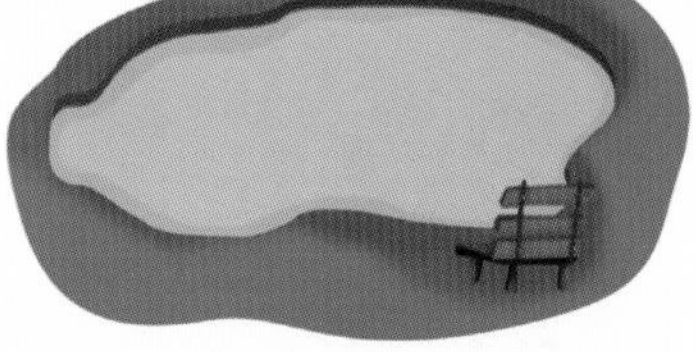

озеро

ozero

lamb

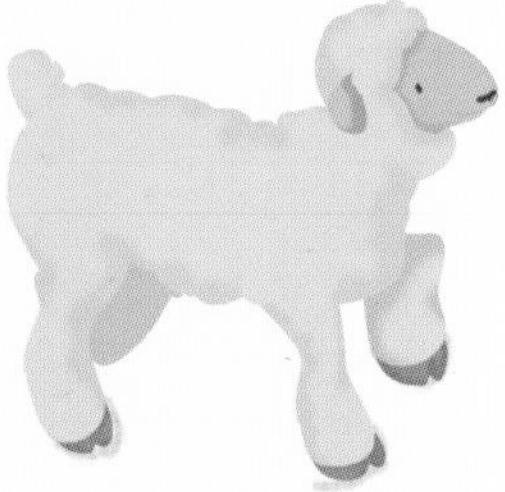

ягня

yahnia

lamp

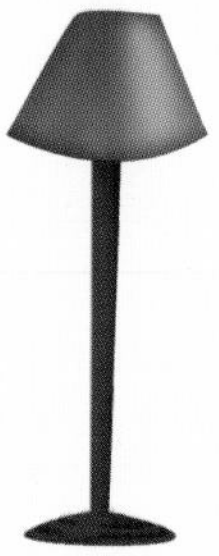

лампа

lampa

lamp post

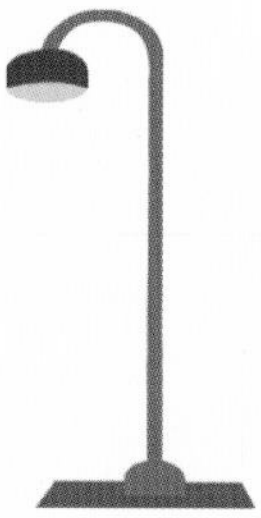

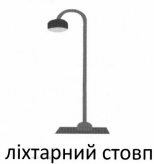

ліхтарний стовп

likhtarnyi stovp

land

земля

zemlia

lane

дорога

doroha

lantern

ліхтар

likhtar

laser

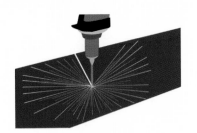

лазер

lazer

lasso

ласо

laso

latch

засувка

zasuvka

laundry

прання

prannia

lawn

газон

hazon

lawyer

юрист

yuryst

layer

шар

shar

leaf

лист

lyst

leather

шкіра

shkira

a
b
c
d
e
f
g
h
i
J
k
l
m
n
o
p
q
r
s
t
u
v
w
x
y
z

a
b
c
d
e
f
g
h
i
J
k
l
m
n
o
p
q
r
s
t
u
v
w
x
y
z

leg

нога

noha

lemon

лимон

lymon

lemonade

лимонад

lymonad

lens

лінза

linza

leopard

леопард

leopard

letter

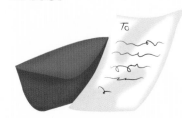

лист

lyst

letterbox
US English **mailbox**

поштова скринька

poshtova skrynka

lettuce

латук

latuk

library

бібліотека

biblioteka

licence

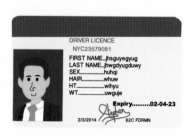

посвідчення

posvidchennia

lid

кришка

kryshka

light

світло

svitlo

lighthouse

маяк

maiak

limb

кінцівка

kintsivka

line

лінія

liniia

lion

лев

lev

lip

губа

huba

lipstick

помада

pomada

liquid

рідина

ridyna

list

перелік

perelik

litre
US English **liter**

літр

litr

living room

вітальня

vitalnia

lizard

ящірка

yashchirka

load

вантаж

vantazh

a b c d e f g h i j k **l** m n o p q r s t u v w x y z

a
b
c
d
e
f
g
h
i
J
k
l
m
n
o
p
q
r
s
t
u
v
w
x
y
z

loaf

хлібина

khlibyna

lobster

лобстер

lobster

lock

замок

zamok

loft

горище

horyshche

log

поліно

polino

loop

петля

petlia

lorry

US English **truck**

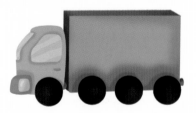

вантажівка

vantazhivka

lotus

лотос

lotos

louse

воша

vosha

luggage

багаж

bahazh

lunch

обід

obid

lung

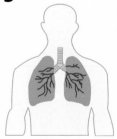

легені

leheni

Mm

machine
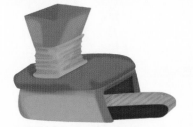
машина
mashyna

magazine

журнал
zhurnal

magician

чарівник
charivnyk

magnet

магніт
mahnit

magpie

сорока
soroka

mail

пошта
poshta

mammal

ссавець
ssavets

man

чоловік
cholovik

mandolin

мандоліна
mandolina

mango

манго
manho

map

мапа
mapa

a b c d e f g h i j k l m n o p q r s t u v w x y z

maple

клен

klen

marble

скляна кулька

skliana kulka

market

ринок

rynok

mask

маска

maska

mast

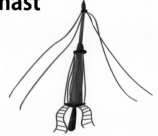

щогла

shchohla

mat

килимок

kylymok

matchbox

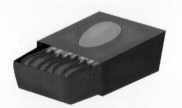

коробка сірників

korobka sirnykiv

mattress

матрац

matrats

meal

блюдо

bliudo

meat

м'ясо

m'iaso

mechanic

механік

mekhanik

medicine

ліки

liky

melon

диня

dynia

merchant

продавець

prodavets

mermaid

русалка

rusalka

metal

метал

metal

metre
US English **meter**

метр

metr

microphone

мікрофон

mikrofon

microwave

мікрохвильова піч

mikrokhvylova pich

mile

миля

mylia

milk

молоко

moloko

miner

шахтар

shakhtar

mineral

мінерал

mineral

mint

м'ята

m'iata

a b c d e f g h i j k l **m** n o p q r s t u v w x y z

minute

хвилина

khvylyna

mirror

дзеркало

dzerkalo

mobile phone

мобільний телефон

mobilnyi telefon

model

модель

model

mole

кріт

krit

money

гроші

hroshi

monk

монах

monakh

monkey

мавпа

mavpa

monster

монстр

monstr

month

місяць

misiats

monument

пам'ятник

pam'iatnyk

moon

місяць

misiats

mop

швабра

shvabra

morning

ранок

ranok

mosquito

комар

komar

moth

міль

mil

mother

мати

maty

motorcycle

мотоцикл

mototsykl

motorway

траса

trasa

mountain

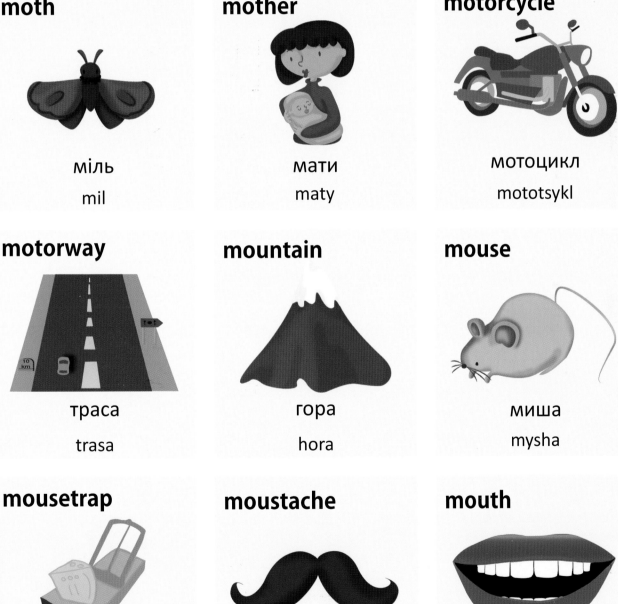

гора

hora

mouse

миша

mysha

mousetrap

мишоловка

mysholovka

moustache

вуса

vusa

mouth

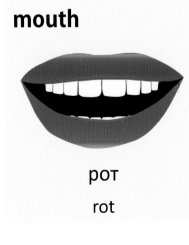

рот

rot

mud

ґрунт

grunt

muffin

кекс

keks

mug

кухоль

kukhol

mule

мул

mul

muscle

м'яз

m'iaz

museum

музей

muzei

mushroom

гриб

hryb

music

музика

muzyka

musician

музикант

muzykant

Nn

nail

цвях

tsviakh

napkin
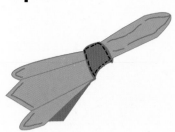

серветка

servetka

nappy
US English **diaper**

підгузок

pidhuzok

nature

природа

pryroda

neck

шия

shyia

necklace

намисто

namysto

necktie

краватка

kravatka

needle

голка

holka

neighbour
US English **neighbor**

сусід

susid

nest

гніздо

hnizdo

net

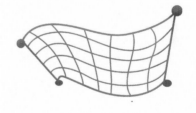

сітка

sitka

newspaper

газета

hazeta

night

ніч

nich

nine

дев'ять

dev'iat

noodles

локшина

lokshina

noon

місяць

misiats

north

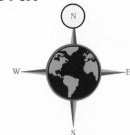

північ

pivnich

nose

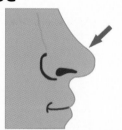

ніс

nis

note

записка

zapyska

notebook

записник

zapysnyk

notice

пам'ятка

pam'iatka

number

0 1 2 3

число

chyslo

nun

черниця

chernytsia

nurse

медсестра

medsestra

nursery

дитяча кімната

dytiacha kimnata

nut

горіх

horikh

Oo

oar

весло

veslo

observatory

обсерваторія

observatoriia

ocean

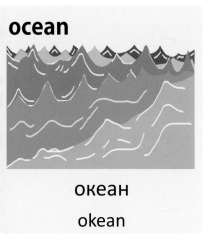

океан

okean

octopus

восьминіг

vosmynih

office

офіс

ofis

oil

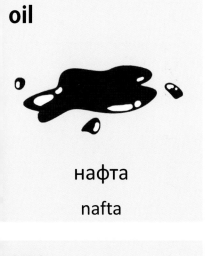

нафта

nafta

olive

олива

olyva

omelette

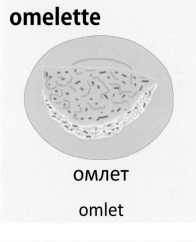

омлет

omlet

one

один

odyn

onion

цибуля

tsybulia

orange

апельсин

apelsyn

orbit
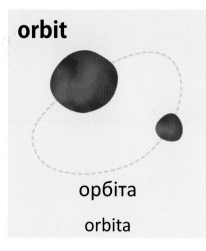
орбіта

orbita

orchard

фруктовий сад

fruktovyi sad

orchestra

оркестр

orkestr

ostrich
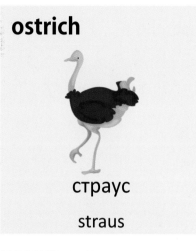
страус

straus

otter
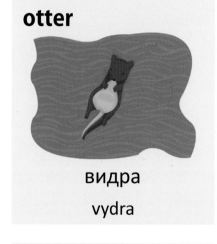
видра

vydra

oval
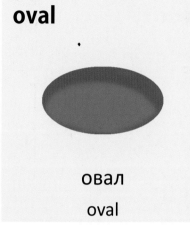
овал

oval

oven
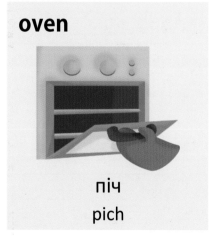
піч

pich

owl

сова

sova

ox

віл

vil

Pp

packet

пакет

paket

page

сторінка

storinka

pain

біль

bil

paint

фарба

farba

painting

живопис

zhyvopys

pair

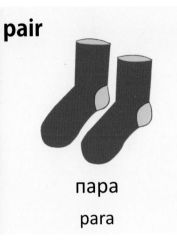

пара

para

palace

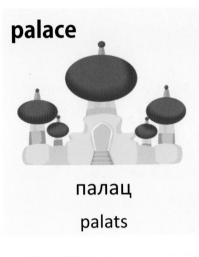

палац

palats

palm

долоня

dolonia

pan

сковорода

skovoroda

pancake

млинці

mlyntsi

panda

панда

panda

papaya

папайя

papaiia

paper

папір

papir

parachute

парашут

parashut

a b c d e f g h i j k l m n o p q r s t u v w x y z

parcel

пакунок

pakunok

park

парк

park

parrot

папуга

papuha

passenger

пасажир

pasazhyr

pasta

макарони

makarony

pastry

кондитерські вироби

kondyterski vyroby

pavement

тротуар

trotuar

paw

лапа

lapa

pea

горох

horokh

peach

персик

persyk

peacock

пава

pava

peak

пік

pik

peanut

арахіс

arakhis

pear

груша

hrusha

pearl

перлина

perlyna

pedal

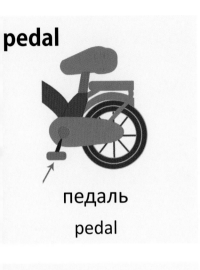

педаль

pedal

pelican

пелікан

pelikan

pen

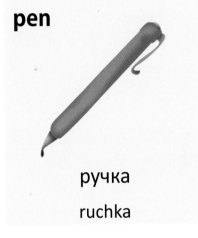

ручка

ruchka

pencil

олівець

olivets

penguin

пінгвін

pinhvin

pepper

перець

perets

perfume

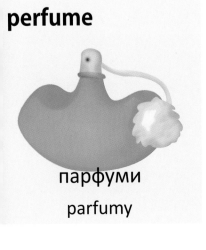

парфуми

parfumy

pet

домашній улюбленець

domashnii uliublenets

pharmacy

аптека

apteka

photograph

фотографія

fotohrafiia

piano

піаніно

pianino

picture

картина

kartyna

pie

пиріг

pyrih

pig

свиня

svynia

pigeon

голуб

holub

pillar
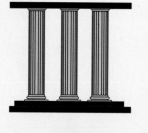
стовп

stovp

pillow

подушка

podushka

pilot

пілот

pilot

pineapple

ананас

ananas

pink

рожевий колір

rozhevyi kolir

pipe

труба

truba

pizza

піцца

pitstsa

planet

планета

planeta

plant

рослина

roslyna

plate

тарілка

tarilka

platform

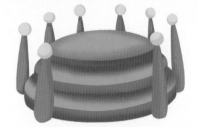

платформа

platforma

platypus

качкодзьоб

kachkodzob

player

гравець

hravets

plum

слива

slyva

plumber

сантехнік

santekhnik

plywood

фанера

fanera

pocket

кишеня

kyshenia

poet

поет

poet

polar bear

полярний ведмідь

poliarnyi vedmid

police

поліція

politsiia

pollution

забруднення

zabrudnennia

pomegranate

гранат

hranat

pond

ставок

stavok

porcupine

дикобраз

dykobraz

port

порт

port

porter

швейцар

shveitsar

postcard

листівка

lystivka

postman

поштар

poshtar

post office

пошта

poshta

pot

горщик

horshchyk

potato

картопля

kartoplia

powder

пудра

pudra

prawn
US English **shrimp**

креветка

krevetka

priest

священик

sviashchenyk

prince

принц

prynts

prison

в'язниця

v'iaznytsia

pudding

пудинг

pudynh

pump

помпа

pompa

pumpkin

гарбуз

harbuz

puppet

маріонетка

marionetka

puppy

цуценя

tsutsenia

purse

гаманець

hamanets

a
b
c
d
e
f
g
h
i
J
K
l
m
n
o
p
q
r
s
t
u
v
w
x
y
z

Qq

quail

перепел

perepel

quarry

кар'єр

kar'ier

queen

королева

koroleva

queue

черга

cherha

quiver

колчан

kolchan

Rr

rabbit

кролик

krolyk

rack

стелаж

stelazh

racket

ракетка

raketka

radio

радіо

radio

radish

редис

redys

raft

пліт

plit

rain

дощ

doshch

rainbow

райдуга

raiduha

raisin

родзинка

rodzynka

ramp

рампа

rampa

raspberry

малина

malyna

rat

щур

shchur

razor

бритва

brytva

receipt

чек

chek

rectangle

прямокутник

priamokutnyk

red

червоний колір

chervonyi kolir

restaurant

ресторан

restoran

a b c d e f g h i j J k l m n o p q r s t u v w x y z

rhinoceros

носоріг

nosorih

rib

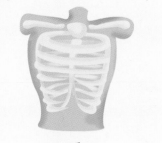

ребро

rebro

ribbon

стрічка

strichka

rice

рис

rys

ring

кільце

kiltse

river

річка

richka

road

дорога

doroha

robber

крадій

kradii

robe

халат

khalat

robot

робот

robot

rock

камінь

kamin

rocket

ракета

raketa

roller coaster

американські гірки

amerykanski hirky

room

кімната

kimnata

root

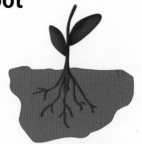

коріння

korinnia

rope

мотузка

motuzka

rose

троянда

troianda

round

коло

kolo

rug

килим

kylym

rugby

регбі

rehbi

ruler

лінійка

liniika

Ss

sack

мішок

mishok

sail

вітрило

vitrylo

abcdefghijklmnopqr**s**tuvwxyz

sailor

моряк

moriak

salad

салат

salat

salt

сіль

sil

sand
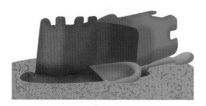
пісок

pisok

sandwich

сандвіч

sandvich

satellite

супутник

suputnyk

saucer

соусник

sousnyk

sausage

сосиска

sosyska

saw

пилка

pylka

scarf

шарф

sharf

school
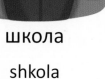
школа

shkola

scissors

ножиці

nozhytsi

scooter

самокат

samokat

scorpion

скорпіон

skorpion

screw

шуруп

shurup

sea

море

more

seal

тюлень

tiulen

seat

крісло

krislo

see-saw

гойдалка

hoidalka

seven

сім

sim

shadow

тінь

tin

shampoo

шампунь

shampun

shark

акула

akula

sheep

вівця

vivtsia

shelf

полиця

polytsia

shell

мушля

mushlia

shelter

укриття

ukryttia

ship

корабель

korabel

shirt

сорочка

sorochka

shoe

черевик

cherevyk

shorts

шорти

shorty

shoulder

плече

pleche

shower

душ

dush

shutter

жалюзі

zhaliuzi

shuttlecock

волан

volan

signal

світлофор

svitlofor

silver

срібло

sriblo

sink

рукомийник

rukomyinyk

sister

сестра

sestra

six

шість

shist

skate

ковзан

kovzan

skeleton

скелет

skelet

ski

лижі

lyzhi

skin

шкіра

shkira

skirt

спідниця

spidnytsia

skull

череп

cherep

sky

небо

nebo

skyscraper

хмарочос

khmarochos

slide

гірка

hirka

slipper

капці

kaptsi

smoke

дим

dym

snail

равлик

ravlyk

snake

змія

zmiia

snow
снiг

snih

soap

мило

mylo

sock

шкарпетка

shkarpetka

sofa

диван

dyvan

soil

ґрунт

grunt

soldier

солдат

soldat

soup
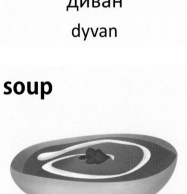
суп

sup

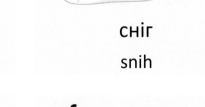

space

космос

kosmos

spaghetti

спагеті

spaheti

sphere

сфера

sfera

spider

павук

pavuk

spinach

шпинат

shpynat

sponge

губка

hubka

spoon

ложка

lozhka

spray

аерозоль

aerozol

spring

весна

vesna

square

квадрат

kvadrat

squirrel

білка

bilka

stadium

Стадіон

Stadion

stairs

сходи

skhody

stamp

марка

marka

star

зірка

zirka

station

станція

stantsiia

statue

статуя

statuia

stethoscope

стетоскоп

stetoskop

stomach
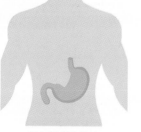
шлунок

shlunok

stone

каміння

kaminnia

storm

шторм

shtorm

straw

соломинка

solomynka

strawberry

полуниця

polunytsia

street

вулиця

vulytsia

student

студент

student

submarine

субмарина

submaryna

subway

метро

metro

sugar

цукор

tsukor

sugarcane

цукрова тростина

tsukrova trostyna

summer

літо

lito

sun

сонце

sontse

supermarket

супермаркет

supermarket

swan

лебідь

lebid

sweet

солодощі

solodoshchi

swimming pool

басейн

basein

swimsuit

купальник

kupalnyk

a b c d e f g h i j J k l m n o p q r **s** t u v w x y z

swing

гойдалка

hoidalka

switch

вимикач

vymykach

syrup

сироп

syrop

Tt

table

стіл

stil

tall

високий ріст

vysokyi rist

tank

танк

tank

taxi

таксі

taksi

tea

чай

chai

teacher

учитель

uchytel

teeth

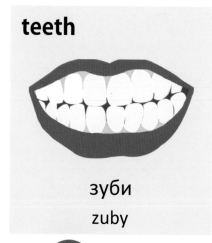

зуби

zuby

telephone

телефон

telefon

television

телебачення

telebachennia

ten

десять

desiat

tennis

теніс

tenis

tent

намет

namet

thief

крадій

kradii

thread
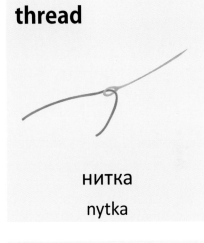
нитка

nytka

three

три

try

throat
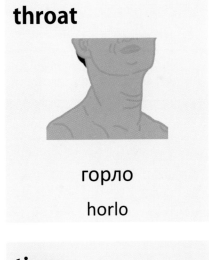
горло

horlo

thumb

великий палець

velykyi palets

ticket

квиток

kvytok

tiger

тигр

tyhr

toe
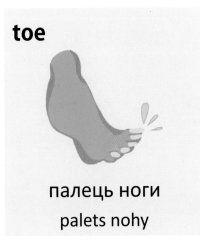
палець ноги

palets nohy

tofu

тофу

tofu

tomato

томат

tomat

tongue

язик

yazyk

tool

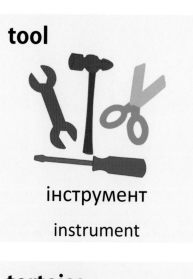

інструмент

instrument

toothbrush

зубна щітка

zubna shchitka

toothpaste

зубна паста

zubna pasta

tortoise

черепаха

cherepakha

towel

рушник

rushnyk

tower

вежа

vezha

toy

іграшка

ihrashka

tractor

трактор

traktor

train

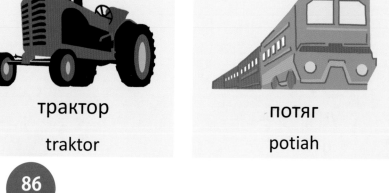

потяг

potiah

tree

дерево

derevo

triangle

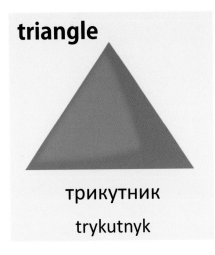

трикутник

trykutnyk

tub

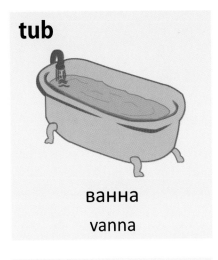

ванна

vanna

tunnel

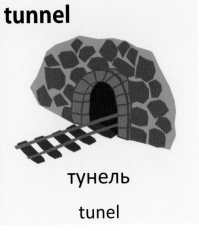

тунель

tunel

turnip

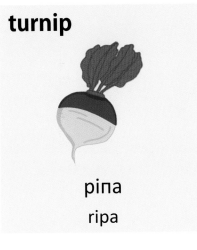

ріпа

ripa

tyre
US English **tire**

шина

shyna

Uu

umbrella

парасолька

parasolka

uncle

дядько

diadko

uniform

уніформа

uniforma

university

університет

universytet

utensil

посуд

posud

Vv

vacuum cleaner

пилосос

pylosos

valley

долина

dolyna

van

фургон

furhon

vase

ваза

vaza

vault

бункер

bunker

vegetable

овоч

ovoch

veil

вуаль

vual

vet

ветеринар

veterynar

village

село

selo

violet

бузковий колір

buzkovyi kolir

violin

скрипка

skrypka

volcano

вулкан

vulkan

volleyball

волейбол

voleibol

vulture

стерв'ятник

sterv'iatnyk

Ww

waist

талія

taliia

waitress

офіціантка

ofitsiantka

wall

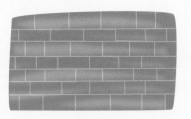

стіна

stina

wallet

гаманець

hamanets

walnut

волоський горіх

voloskyi horikh

wand

чарівна паличка

charivna palychka

wardrobe

шафа

shafa

warehouse

склад

sklad

a b c d e f g h i J k l m n o p q r s t u v w x y z

wasp

оса

osa

watch

годинник

hodynnyk

water

вода

voda

watermelon

кавун

kavun

web

павутиння

pavutynnia

whale

кит

kyt

wheat

пшениця

pshenytsia

wheel

колесо

koleso

whistle

свисток

svystok

white

білий колір

bilyi kolir

wife

дружина

druzhyna

window

вікно

vikno

wing

крило

krylo

winter

зима

zyma

wizard

чаклун

chaklun

wolf

вовк

vovk

woman

жінка

zhinka

woodpecker

дятел

diatel

wool

вовна

vovna

workshop
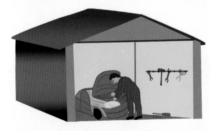
майстерня

maisternia

wrist

зап'ястя

zap'iastia

x-ray
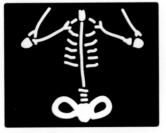
рентген

renthen

xylophone

ксилофон

ksylofon

a b c d e f g h i J k l m n o p q r s t u v w x y z

a b c d e f g h i J k l m n o p q r s t u v w x y z

Yy

yacht

яхта

yakhta

yak

як

yak

yard

подвір'я

podvir'ia

yellow

жовтий колір

zhovtyi kolir

yoghurt

йогурт

yohurt

Zz

zebra

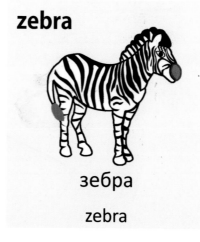

зебра

zebra

zero

нуль

nul

zip

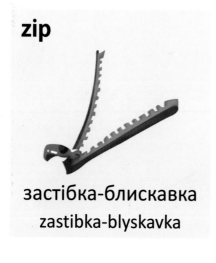

застібка-блискавка

zastibka-blyskavka

zodiac

зодіак

zodiak

zoo

зоопарк

zoopark